MANY VERSES!

THE IMPORTANCE OF READING THE SCRIPTURES IN REFORMED WORSHIP

By Ernest Springer

With An Appendix Containing Historical Narrative
And Debate At The Westminster Assembly of Divines

Foreword by Dr. Frank J. Smith
Minister of Affirmation Presbyterian Church
Lincolndale, NY

Old Paths Publications
Ernie Springer
223 Princeton Road
Audubon, NJ 08106
...ask for the old paths... Jer. 6:16

Old Paths First Edition 1993

ISBN 0-9632557-2-X

© Copyright 1993 by Ernest Springer

All rights reserved. No part of this publication may be reproduced, stored in a retrieval system, or transmitted, in any form or by any means, electronic, mechanical, photocopying, recording, or otherwise, without the prior permission of Old Paths Publications. As an exception, permission is hereby granted for reprinting excerpts in periodicals or as part of a book review, provided that proper acknowledgment is given, and that a copy of the periodical in which such review appears is sent to Old Paths Publications.

Foreword

© Copyright 1993 by Dr. Frank J. Smith

On the front cover: Ancient Jewish Synagogue (Courtesy of The Christian Observer)

DEDICATION

This book is dedicated to my wife and children that they may always "*Seek ye out of the book of the Lord and read.*"

ACKNOWLEDGMENT

The author gratefully acknowledges the labors of Mr. Charles Greenewald for his editing, and a number of faithful ministers for their reviews and suggestions. Special thanks is also due Mr. Jeffrey Mumma and Mr. Albert Salmon.

...give attendance to reading, to exhortation, to doctrine.

(I Timothy 4:13)

Contents

Foreword	i
Introduction	1
"What Saith the Scripture?"	3
A Low View of Scripture	5
The Error of Arminianism	6
The Error of Dispensationalism	7
"True to the Reformed Faith"	10
The Regulative Principle Guides	11
The Old Testament Still Speaks	18
The Synagogue and the New Testament	23
The Early Church	26
Reformed Tradition	29
Scripture Reading as an Element of Worship Today	34
Why Has There Been a Decline in Reading?	42
Modern Versions and Paraphrases	43
The Scourge of the Charismatic and Pentecostal Movements	46
The Acceptance of Unbelievers in the Churches	47
Objections Considered	50
Pragmatism	50
Adiaphora	51
"Bibliolatry!" – The Bible an Idol?	53
An Exhortation	58
Appendix - Historical Narrative and Debate	61

FOREWORD

Many verses! What an odd topic for a booklet. Why in the world would it matter how much Scripture is read during public worship?

But before this work is dismissed as obscurantist, let me urge the reader to consider the fact that the Bible is the very Word of God. It is hence inerrant, infallible, and inspired, and its character alone should command respect. But more than that, it is God's special revelation, particularly to His covenant people—a love letter, as it were, conveying in a variety of ways the Lord's intense desire for union with His elect.

In a direct manner, we who have been chosen from eternity have the opportunity to hear from our God's own lips all He wants us to know. In historical narrative, in poetry, in prose, in prophetic utterance, God speaks—and He speaks to us.

This is not a privilege lightly foregone. Yet in a day when believers in formerly Communist countries are finally able to engage in public worship without fear of reprisal, we in North America are facing a time when the divine vision is indeed becoming rare—even in churches that are professedly evangelical and/or Reformed.

Perhaps it is because we don't believe the Bible anymore or don't take God seriously. Maybe it is because we don't want to wrestle with various portions of the Bible which we have trouble understanding or because we don't want to be humble before a God Who speaks in particular ways. Perchance we're embarrassed by many of the inspired accounts—not just the content but the fact that they're there, or by certain expressions which seem irrelevant (such as "Selah" or the titles in the Psalms).

Whatever the cause, it is clear that we need an acknowledgement of the transcendent in our worship. One of the most crucial ways for that to occur is by an abundant reading of Heaven's communication to us.

Ernie Springer is to be commended for this courageous, forthright polemic in favor of the historic practice of feeding the flock with "many verses." May the God of Scripture be pleased to bless this book to the end that every Lord's Day, the officers of the church will not refrain from reading publicly much material from the Word.

                    Frank J. Smith, Ph. D.
                    Somers, New York
                    October 31, 1992

INTRODUCTION

Something terrible is happening to the worship of God in many churches which claim to be true to the Holy Scriptures and to the Reformed Faith. It is something of which the average church member might not even be aware. It is not as noticeable as the inclusion of women in church office, the use of solos accompanied by booming contemporary music, clapping, drama presentations, joking and laughter from the pulpit, liturgical dance and congregational applause. No, it is much more subtle than these. In fact, it is not the addition of anything. Rather, it is the subtraction, or *diminishing*, of a vital component of Reformed and Biblical worship – the public reading of God's Holy Word.

Few people who claim to adhere to the tenets of the Reformed Faith, as set forth in the *Westminster Confession of Faith and Catechisms*, *Belgic Confession*, *Heidelberg Catechism*, and the *Canons of Dordt*, would deny the truth that the Scriptures are a means of grace unto salvation, and the reading and faithful preaching of them are ways in which God speaks to, and opens, the hearts of unsaved men, women and children. And it is through the reading and faithful preaching of the Word that God edifies and comforts His elect. The Scriptures not only reveal the will of God, but they also reveal to us the very persons of the Godhead. In the Scriptures, God reveals Himself as the faithful, triune covenant God who saves His people from their sins. The Scriptures are not a jumbled collection of idealistic stories which contain some "gems" of wisdom for our casual reflection. Instead, they are the utterances of the Holy Spirit — the very words of God Himself, spoken and written down by holy men of God *"as they were moved by the Holy Ghost"* (II Peter 1:21). Through the Scriptures, the Holy Spirit commands us to obedience, convicts us of our sinfulness, and communicates His saving grace and direction for our lives.

    This being said, let us be mindful of man's chief end — to glorify God and to enjoy Him forever.

"WHAT SAITH THE SCRIPTURE?"

Because it is the Holy Spirit who has authored the Scriptures, the importance of the Word of God to its reader or hearer is a spiritual matter. In any discussion of spiritual matters, the question to be asked is, *"For what saith the Scripture?"* (Romans 4:3). The Bible has a great deal to say about itself, particularly about the effect it has on the one who reads, hears or sits under its faithful and diligent exposition:

* Psa. 119:105: *"Thy word is a lamp unto my feet and a light unto my path."*

* Psa. 119:130: *"The entrance of thy words giveth light; it giveth understanding unto the simple."*

* Luke 11:28: *"Blessed are they that hear the word of God, and keep it."*

* Rom. 10:17: *"So then faith cometh by hearing, and hearing by the word of God."*

* I Thes. 2:13: *"It is in truth, the word of God, which effectually worketh also in you that believe."*

* Heb. 4:12: *"For the word of God is quick, and powerful, and sharper than any twoedged sword, piercing even to the dividing asunder of soul and spirit, and of the joints and marrow, and is a discerner of the thoughts and intents of the heart."*

* James 1:21: *"Wherefore lay apart all filthiness and superfluity of naughtiness, and receive with meekness the engrafted word, which is able to save your souls."*

> * I Pet. 2:2: *"As newborn babes, desire the sincere milk of the word, that ye may grow thereby."*

Certainly, these verses are a strong testimony to the importance of the Word of God for its recipients.

A LOW VIEW OF SCRIPTURE

There have been many movements and trends throughout Protestantism over the last hundred years that have precipitated a noticeable decline in the high view of Scripture once held by the church; trends that have undermined the Christian faith and have contributed to the increasing abandonment of God's Word. Modern scientific and theological theories have tickled the ears of so many in our day, causing them to reject the creation account of the book of Genesis, the existence of the Creator Himself, the totally depraved condition of natural man and his need for a savior, and a whole host of doctrines once embraced by Reformed believers since the Reformation. Ultimately, erroneous modernist theories – spawned in unbelief – have cast a dark shadow upon the inerrancy of God's Word, which lights the path of the child of God (Psa. 119:105, 130). Hence, regard for the hearing of the Scriptures becomes a regard for what is perceived to be merely the words of mortal men. The eye-opening declaration that causes squirming in the pews, "Thus **saith** the LORD," has been replaced with a casual "Thus *meaneth* the LORD." The very words of God Almighty are no longer the standard of excellence. They are not in the memory of the listener, their sound is unfamiliar, and the listener sits in spiritual decay asking, "Is that all there is?" and "What **is** truth, anyway?"

In addition, significant doctrinal errors have

contributed to the decline in how churches view the Word of God. Some of these errors, while appearing to be new, are in actuality old heresies under the cloak of new names. As two of these errors are briefly cited here, and two others further on, they should not be viewed as being exclusive of one another. Rather, they should be understood as being interwoven, and in some ways proceeding from one another. Moreover, *all of them* in some fashion bring people to question the absolute sovereignty of God and His Word, and to embrace — as from the beginning — **the lie** (Genesis 3:1-4).

The Error of Arminianism

Arminianism, which is replete with errors and heresies, encourages subtle yet significant de-emphatic tendencies toward the Scriptures. Closely resembling the age-old heresy of Pelagianism, it defends the autonomy of man by setting him up against the absolute sovereignty of God. Because the emphatic truths of God's eternal predestination, His sovereign election, and His Covenant of Grace run throughout the Scriptures, the Arminian will wrongly divide and do violence to the Word. Many passages which contain spiritual truth stay forever buried in the infinite mines of the Bible. Hence the deep things of God, the splendor of His majesty, the power of His sovereignty, and the everlasting wealth of the Gospel of Grace remain hidden from the Arminian, never to stir his heart into a longing for more — much more. Not only does Arminianism give rise to other errors, but whenever one begins to question the absolute sovereignty of God, one in some sense (perhaps unknowingly and unintentionally) relegates the Word of God to a place of insignificance. Hence, the Arminian falls into the deadly trap of listening to and believing **the lie**.

The Error of Dispensationalism[1]

Dispensationalism openly denies the applicability – and hence, the importance – of the majority of the Bible to the believer today. Many books, many passages, and *many verses* in the Bible are seen as merely history, about irrelevant events; worn-out relics of a bygone era. Dispensationalists fail to see the Scriptures as a cohesive and continuous whole. They fail to realize that the Scriptures speak of the one, true God who changes not. They disassociate the Gospel from the Old Testament saints, when Scripture states to the contrary, *"For unto us was the gospel preached, as well as unto them"* (Heb. 4:2).

The Old Testament Scriptures, which demonstrate the importance of God's moral laws, show the disobedience by many people of His commands and tell of His judgment and wrath against sinful and rebellious man, are often disregarded and laid aside without application.

---

[1] These errors (Arminianism and Dispensationalism) can, and in some cases do, contribute to a lack of appreciation for the written Word of God and often result in a lack of desire to read it and hear it read. This is not to say that, as a rule, all Arminian and Dispensational congregations read small amounts of Scripture. However, as today's worship practices grow more and more man-centered, man-directed and experiential (or emotionalistic), there is a decline because they are losing (and may have lost) their first love, Jesus Christ, the Word made flesh.

And this, in spite of I Corinthians 10:6 and 11 which clearly say, *"Now these things were our examples, to the intent we should not lust after evil things, as they also lusted,"* and *"Now all these things happened unto them for ensamples: and they are written for our admonition, upon whom the ends of the world are come."* These explanations by the apostle Paul of the applicability of Old Testament Scripture to New Testament times is not uncommon, as also seen in Romans 4:23-24: *"Now it was not written for his sake alone...But for us also..."*; I Corinthians 9:9-10: *"For it is written in the law of Moses...For our sakes, no doubt, this is written..."*; and Romans 15:4: *"For whatsoever things were written aforetime were written for our learning, that we through patience and comfort of the scriptures might have hope."* So, the sad result is men, women and children who are ignorantly instructed to remain unmoved by the hearing of Old Testament Scripture. By this neglect of Scripture, they deprive themselves of patience, comfort and hope of the Gospel. They have, instead, embraced **the lie**.

But our souls are to be nourished by the *entire* Word of God. It is this Word which makes our way plain and leads us in the paths of righteousness. It is the law of our life, a bounty of instruction. In our times of joy, it directs our glorying to the Father from whom all blessings flow. In our times of distress, God is shown to be our help in ages past, our refuge in times of trouble, our high tower and sure defense from the enemy. As a comprehensive guide for our lives we find that "The Bible reveals the mind of God, the state of man, the way of salvation, the doom of sinners, and the happiness of believers. Its doctrines are holy, its precepts are binding, its histories true, and its decisions are unchangeable. Read it to be wise, believe it to be safe, and practise it to be holy. It contains light to direct you, food to support you, and comfort to cheer you. It is the traveller's map, the pilgrim's staff, the pilot's compass, the soldier's sword, and the Christian's charter. Here Paradise is restored, Heaven opened, and the gates of Hell disclosed. CHRIST is its GRAND SUBJECT, our good its design, and the glory of God its end. It should fill the memory, rule the heart, and guide the feet. Read it slowly, frequently, and prayerfully. It is a mine of wealth, a paradise of glory, and a river of pleasure. It is given you in life, will be opened in the Judgment, and will be remembered forever. It involves the highest responsibility, rewards the greatest labour, and condemns all who trifle with its holy contents."[2]

So then, as II Timothy 3:16-17 says, *"All scripture is given by inspiration of God, and is profitable for doctrine, for reproof, for correction, for instruction in righteousness: That the man of God may be perfect, throughly furnished unto all good works."*

---

[2]Rev. W. MacLean, *The Providential Preservation of the Greek Text of the New Testament* (Gisbourne, Westminster Standard, 1977), pp. 29-30.

"True to the Reformed Faith"

How, then, are we to relate the importance the Scriptures claim for themselves to the Reformed faith? If a church is to honor its profession of being true to the Reformed faith, then the leadership of that church must know and embrace those things which make that church distinctively **Reformed**. A high view of the Scriptures is just such a distinctive. The Reformed minister and elder must be able to teach faithfully and defend both doctrine and practice from the Scriptures. The importance of learning doctrine and practice from the Scriptures is one of the strongest messages of the Reformation. Do the leaders of the church know the Scriptures? Do they teach them to their children? Could they teach them to adults? Could they defend – from the Scriptures – the Reformed faith against Pelagian and Arminian heresy? The Lord Jesus Christ, in dealing with the spiritual leaders of His day, had many things to say to them, but He struck at the root of their problem with His statements, *"Have ye never read..."*, *"Did ye never read in the scriptures..."*, and *"Ye do err, not knowing the scriptures..."* (Matt. 21:16,42; 22:29).

This naturally brings us to the subject of the sufficiency of the Scriptures as the regulatory means for the life of the believer. Even more specifically, it is the Word of God which is the sole and sufficient authority for guidance and direction in our worship of God.

THE REGULATIVE PRINCIPLE GUIDES

What is worship? Simply stated, worship is our response to God's revelation of His glory. In the corporate, visible body, specific worship is done in God's *special presence*, through the reading, and especially the preaching of the Word. The Word reveals God's glory, and once confronted with God's glory, we must worship. Moses requested to be shown God's glory; his request was answered, and at once Moses worshiped (cf. Ex. 33:18; 34:5-7). Therefore the Scriptures are always essential to worship.

What has come to be known as the Regulative Principle of Worship is a principle presented in the Scriptures (Gen. 4:3-7; Ex. 20:4-6; 25:40; Lev. 10:1-3; Deut. 4:2; 12:32; I Sam. 13:11ff; I Ki. 12:32-33; I Chr. 15:13; II Chr. 26:16; Jer. 7:31; Matt. 15:9; Matt. 28:19-20; John 4:22-24; Acts 17:23-25; Col. 2:18-23). It teaches that we are to worship God only in ways He commands in His Word. We are not to insert into the worship service any elements which are the fabrications and inventions of man. God is honored *only* when we worship Him according to means set forth in His Word (either by direct commandment or logical implication), and when we do not add to or take away from anything set forth therein.

That this is the historical Reformed position can be seen clearly in the Reformed confessions and catechisms. The *Belgic Confession* (1561), Article VII, speaking on the sufficiency of the Holy Scriptures as the only rule of faith, states:

> We believe that these Holy Scriptures fully contain the will of God... the whole manner of worship which God requires of us is written in them... Neither may we consider any writings of men, though ever so holy, with those divine Scriptures; nor ought we to compare custom, or the great multitude, or antiquity, or succession of times or persons, or councils, decrees, or statutes, with the truth of God, for the truth is above all.[3]

Further, in Article XXXII of the same document, entitled "Of the Order and Discipline of the Church" appears the following statement:

> Those who are rulers of the church...ought studiously to take care that they do not depart from those things which Christ, our only Master, hath instituted. And therefore, we reject all human inventions, and all laws which man would introduce into the worship of God.[4]

The *Heidelberg Catechism* (1563) also gives testimony to the Regulative Principle of Worship in Question and Answer 96:

> Q: What does God require in the second commandment?
> A: That we in nowise make any image of God, nor worship him in any other way than he has commanded in his Word.[5]

---

[3] Philip Schaff, Ed., *The Creeds of Christendom*, Volume III, "The Evangelical Creeds" (Grand Rapids, Baker Book House, 1990, Reprinted from Harper & Row's 1931 edition), pp. 387-388.

[4] *Ibid*, p. 423.

[5] *Ibid*, p. 343.

Speaking of the service of God, the *Irish Articles of Religion* (1615), Article 52, states:

> All worship devised by man's phantasy besides or contrary to the Scriptures...hath not only no reward of Scripture, but contrariwise threatenings and maledictions.⁶

Looking at the Presbyterian Churches, we find the same truth taught in Answers 109 and 51, respectively, of the *Westminster Larger and Shorter Catechisms* (1647):

> The sins forbidden in the second commandment are, all devising, counseling, commanding, using, and anywise approving, any religious worship not instituted by God himself...corrupting the worship of God, adding to it, or taking from it, whether invented and taken up of ourselves, or received by tradition from others, though under the title of antiquity, custom, devotion, good intent, or any other pretense whatsoever.
>
> The second commandment forbiddeth the worshiping of God by images, or any way not appointed in his Word.⁷

The *Westminster Confession of Faith* (1647), Chapter XXI, Section I states:

> But the acceptable way of worshiping the true God is instituted by himself, and so limited to his own revealed will, that he may not be worshiped according to the imaginations and devices of men, or the suggestions of Satan, under any visible representations,

---

⁶*Ibid*, p. 536.

⁷*Ibid*, pp. 193-195.

or any other way not prescribed in the Holy Scripture.[8]

The Regulative Principle, therefore, guides us in our worship of God. It is an undeniable fact of Christian history that the approach of the Reformed and Presbyterian churches to the worship of God was to include *only* that which He wills in His Word, and *not* that which He was "silent" about or did not specifically prohibit. The Word of God was not viewed, as it pertained to the essential and substantial elements of worship, as an insufficient collection of partial instructions. Their understanding was as the *Westminster Confession of Faith*, Chapter I, Section IV, declares:

> The whole counsel of God, concerning all things necessary for his own glory, man's salvation, faith, and life, is either expressly set down in Scripture, or by good and necessary consequence may be deduced from Scripture...[9]

In addition to things expressly stated or commanded in the Bible, there are things that are not expressed, but rather logically implied. These things may be inferred from a text by principle or example. The text might not say in so many words, "Thou shalt" or "Thou shalt not," but it might say that "the righteous man does...but the fool does..." Even without a direct command, it is obvious that the believer may never choose the course of a fool. This is what it means to be regulated by Scripture. This is what the *Confession* means when it says that in absence of any express commands, our practices

---

[8]*Ibid*, p. 646.

[9]*Ibid*, p. 603.

"by good and necessary consequence may be deduced from Scripture."

When we examine Reformed worship practices, we see that this is exactly what was done to determine the ordinances of worship. For example, there is no command in Scripture which says, "Thou shalt worship on the Lord's Day, the first day of the week." In fact, the Bible *seems* at first glance to command 7th Day worship and rest. Nevertheless, we worship on the first day of the week (Sunday) because of the Scriptural example of the disciples, who "*...upon the first day of the week...came together to break bread [and] Paul preached unto them...*" (Acts 20:7). We also apply the principle of a "one day in seven" rest established from the creation of this world.

This new Christian Sabbath came into being because the Lord Jesus Christ was resurrected on the first day of the week. Therefore, we meet on the Lord's day to show the fulfillment of the promise of the eternal Sabbath the child of God has in Christ. But there is no direct command in the Bible to do so. There are only examples from which our principles of worship "by good and necessary consequence may be deduced from Scripture."

The Regulative Principle has direct bearing upon every element of a worship service, and that includes the element of the Scripture reading. The *Westminster Confession of Faith*, Chapter XXI, Section V, states, "The reading of the Scriptures with Godly fear [is part] of the ordinary religious worship of God..."[10] If Godly fear is good, and necessary for the corporate reading of God's Word, is it not true then that much reading with much fear is preferable

---

[10]*Ibid*, p. 647.

to little? What place should the reading of Scripture have in our worship? How much of the Word of God should be read in a worship service?

We will not here discuss *who* should read (although given the age in which we live, it is a necessity to state that the minister should ordinarily do the reading); whether there should be exposition[11] or whether to pray before or after the reading. Nor will we consider the *location* in the place of worship from which the readings should be presented. Our attention is only upon the *importance* and the *necessity* of the reading of the Scriptures in the public worship of God. However, to expound further on what was said above regarding the need for preaching, it should be stated that the importance of the sermon is not to be lessened or negated. Rather, it is to be held in the highest regard as the chief means of grace. As the Scriptures testify, God Himself ordained men, *"that he might send them forth to preach"* (Mk. 3:14), that they might go *"everywhere preaching the word"* (Acts 8:4) to them who need to hear, for *"how shall they hear without a preacher?"* (Rom. 10:14). We must echo the sentiment of Isaiah 52:7: *"How beautiful upon the mountains are the feet of him that bringeth good tidings, that publisheth peace; that bringeth good tidings of good, that publisheth salvation; that saith unto Zion, Thy God reigneth!"*

But the intent of this defense of the reading of God's Word in corporate worship is to highlight the reading, not simply as a means of grace in

---

[11] An interesting exchange on the subject of *who* should read the Scripture in public worship, and whether or not it should be done with exposition, is found in the Appendix to this study. These selections have been taken from the Journals and Notes of certain commissioners of the Westminster Assembly.

connection with the greater means of the preaching, but to focus upon the reading as the very foundation and starting point of that preaching, without which there can be no authoritative reference point. Moreover, because the Scriptures are the utterances of the Holy Spirit, by the Spirit's work they speak to us directly and with power. This is something which needs to be emphasized today. The Scriptures do not speak to us through the theologians who interpret them, and they do not speak to us solely through the preacher in the pulpit. Rather, they speak to us in, of, and by themselves.

This can be seen very clearly in the Books of Church Order (BCO) of the Orthodox Presbyterian Church (OPC) and the Presbyterian Church in America (PCA). In their respective "Directories for the Public Worship of God," there are precise and parallel statements dealing with the public reading of the Holy Scriptures. Quoting, then, from the OPC Directory, Chapter III, Article 2:

> The public reading of the Holy Scriptures is performed by the minister as God's servant. Through it God speaks most directly to the congregation, **even more directly than through the interpretation of Holy Writ in the sermon** [Emphasis added].[12]

It should be obvious that the reading of Scripture *must* occupy a position of importance in our worship. But is this understanding rightly applied today? Are the Scriptures viewed as regulatory, and therefore used for the practical

---

[12] Orthodox Presbyterian Church, *The Book of Church Order--The Directory for the Public Worship of God* (Norcross, Great Commission Publications, 1992), p. 220.

outworking of the Scripture reading in the worship service? Can principles regarding the amount of Scripture read "...by good and necessary consequence be deduced from Scripture"?

The Old Testament Still Speaks

There are several Old Testament examples of occasions when Scripture was read in abundance for great periods of time. It is important to understand that many times in the Old Testament when we see expressions such as "the congregation of Israel," "a solemn assembly," or "gathering together as one man," we may conclude that formal gatherings of worship are being described. There are also other expressions which point to the congregational worship of God.

In Joshua 8:34-35, after Joshua built an altar unto the Lord, and burnt offerings and peace offerings were sacrificed (this too constituting worship), we read:

> *And afterward he read all the words of the law, the blessings and cursings, according to all that is written in the book of the law.*[13] *There was not a word of all that Moses commanded, which Joshua read not before all the congregation of Israel, with the women, and the little ones, and the strangers that were conversant among them.*

Clearly, all that Moses commanded, all that is written, all the words of the law, and the blessings and cursings contained in the first five books of the Bible represents an abundance of reading! And

---

[13]In the Old Testament, Moses and other prophets actually wrote the Word of God not chapter by chapter, or book by book, but scroll by scroll. Nevertheless, the word "scroll" (Heb. *sefer*) is rendered "book".

why should it not be so? For when we examine the broader context of this passage, the abundant honoring of God through the hearing of His Word is entirely appropriate given the solemn nature of the event; and the day as the altar was being built, as sacrifices were offered, and as the ark of the covenant was before them – all of this following a glorious victory given them by God over the city of Ai. To put it succinctly, God was **worthy** of such an expression of reverence. Is He less worthy today?

In II Chronicles 34:14ff, we read of the discovery – during the good reign of Josiah – of the long lost *"book of the law of the* LORD *given by Moses."* We find *"when the king had heard the words of the law, that he rent his clothes,"* for he knew of the great wrath of the LORD that should come because his fathers did not keep the Word of the LORD, *"to do after all that is written in this book."* And then we read in verses 29-32:

> *Then the king sent and gathered together all the elders of Judah and Jerusalem. And the king went up into the house of the LORD, and all the men of Judah, and the inhabitants of Jerusalem, and the priests, and the Levites, and all the people, great and small: and he read in their ears all the words of the book of the covenant that was found in the house of the LORD. And the king stood in his place, and made a covenant before the LORD, to walk after the LORD, and to keep his commandments, and his testimonies, and his statutes, with all his heart, and with all his soul, to perform the words of the covenant which are written in this book. And he caused all that were present in Jerusalem and Benjamin to stand to it. And the inhabitants of Jerusalem did according to the covenant of God, the God of their fathers.*

The people of God, both great and small, cannot keep the commandments and statutes of the Lord, nor walk with Him to know His will, without the faithful reading and preaching of God's Word. As the well known Bishop J.C. Ryle said, "Ignorance of the Bible is the root of all error!" One can see that, in all likelihood, the king read in the ears of all the people the words of the book of the covenant in order to bring about in them a national repentance, as was brought about in himself. Furthermore, the people *"departed not from following the LORD"* all of the king's life. It may be that their faithfulness through the years was driven by their regular attentiveness to the Word as they were abundantly exposed to it. Is there a lesser need for repentance among the people of God in these last days?

Nehemiah 8:1-3 gives us a marvelous account of how much God's people love Him, demonstrated by a longing for the reading of His Word. It says:

> *And all the people gathered themselves together as one man into the street that was before the water gate; and they spake unto Ezra the scribe to bring the book of the law of Moses, which the LORD had commanded to Israel. And Ezra the priest brought the law before the congregation both of men and women, and all that could hear with understanding, upon the first day of the seventh month. And he read therein before the street that was before the water gate from the morning until midday, before the men and the women, and those that could understand; and the ears of all the people were attentive unto the book of the law.*

Ezra's reading before the congregation lasted from the morning (literally, "light" or "sunrise" in the Hebrew) until midday! They listened to him read the Word of God for six hours, and were attentive to the reading! We find also in verse 18 of the same chapter that *"day by day from the first day unto the last day, he read in the book of the law of God"* – <u>for seven days</u>! Such was their love of God's Word. In this way they demonstrated their love for

God Himself.

And Nehemiah 9:1-3 reads:

> The children of Israel were assembled with fasting, and with sackclothes, and earth upon them. And the seed of Israel separated themselves from all strangers, and stood and confessed their sins, and the iniquities of their fathers. And they stood up in their place, and read in the book of the law of the LORD their God one fourth part of the day; another fourth part they confessed, and worshipped the LORD their God.

One can only gaze with amazement (and dare I say admiration?) at such a verse as this, and be humbled by the devotion of these people who desired to listen to their God speak AT GREAT LENGTH! This "fourth part of a day" is either 3 or possibly 6 hours. In either case, this assembly for worship lasted twice that time — either 6 or possibly 12 hours! Notice also that these people *stood up in their place* to hear the Word of God read.

Now, these examples are not intended to suggest that the pattern of Scripture reading exhibited in Nehemiah is normative for the regular worship of the church, although great profit would no doubt ensue. And it is not to propose the necessity of mandatory readings of a minimum number of verses, or prescribed periods of time. Nor should it be understood from this passage that God requires *lectio continua* (the continuous or successive reading of passages from one week to the next). However, these Biblical accounts *do* present us with an important and wise example of a people desiring an abundance of truth from the God-built foundation of the Word. While there appears, in at least one of the accounts, to be exposition of the texts given between readings, this does not negate the importance of the actual reading of the Word as a distinct and separate element of the worship service. This is an element greatly neglected in our day.

Moreover, these historical events do not come before us accidentally or incidentally. Rather, the great significance of such piety makes certain and clear for us today that the endurance of the human constitution, the attention of the mind and intellect, and the emotion of the heart, can all cooperatively be brought to bear upon the mandated privilege of sanctifying the name of God in the hearing of the Word.

THE SYNAGOGUE AND THE NEW TESTAMENT

Ezra's reading of the scrolls before the congregation was a precursor to synagogue worship. In the early New Testament church, the primary influence upon these congregations was that of the synagogue[14] with its lectionary readings.[15]

What place did the Scriptures have in the worship in the synagogue? The answer is that the Scriptures occupied a central place. That centrality has been described by Paul Engle as follows:

> This was physically evident because the main article of furniture was a small chest containing scrolls of the Old

---

[14]It is not my intention to enter into a long explanation as to the influence of the Synagogue. However, the reader is encouraged to survey the abundant literature on this subject. One such work is Jacob Mann's, *The Bible as Read and Preached in the Old Synagogue*, 2 vols., New York: KTAV Publishing House, Inc., 1971.

[15]As to the use of a lectionary, I do not believe that the Bible mandates its use. Thus, it is not necessary to advocate its use today. While it does not appear to be prohibited in God's Word, and does not appear to be in conflict with the practices which by good and necessary consequence may be deduced from Scripture, it is something that must be given sufficient thought before institution, for it may not be the wisest practice today, given the nature of abuse and misuse by those seeking a more ceremonially romantic expression of the worship experience.

Testament. It was similar to the ark of the covenant in the tabernacle and the temple containing the stone tablets of God's Law. The synagogue chest reminded people of the importance of God's Word....The high value placed on Scripture was also evident in the use of **seven readings** from the Old Testament in the worship services. A special reading was also given from the Old Testament prophets [Emphasis added].[16]

New Testament examples of Scripture reading in worship demonstrate the regard the people of God had for the pattern previously established. They also serve to reinforce the continuity of the readings from age to age. The regular practice of Scripture reading as an element of worship has not been instituted because of a specific, direct biblical command, but because of the examples of God's people in Scripture. Acts 15:21, a proof used in the *Westminster Confession of Faith* (Chapter XXI, Section V) to support the reading of the Scriptures in Worship, reads, *"For Moses of old time hath in every city them that preach him, being read in the synagogues every sabbath day."* In Acts 13:14-15, the Apostle Paul and those who were with him *"...went into the synagogue on the sabbath day, and sat down. And after the reading of the law and the prophets..."* Again, by Scriptural example, the Lord Jesus Christ *"...as his custom was...went into the synagogue on the sabbath day, and stood up for to read. And there was delivered unto him the book of the prophet Esaias. And when he had opened the book, he found the place where it was*

---

[16]Paul E. Engle, *Discovering the Fullness of Worship* (Philadelphia, Great Commission Publications, 1978), pp. 41, 42.

written..." (Luke 4:16-17).[17]

Each of these passages makes it quite clear (by example, and not by a direct command) that the practice of the reading of Scripture in worship was a regular Sabbath day occurrence. It has been regarded as an element of worship through the ages because it "by good and necessary consequence may be deduced from Scripture."

---

[17] It should be noted, that while the portion of Scripture read by our Lord appears to be relatively small, as seen earlier this was only one of "seven readings." Also, it may very well be that only an ellipsis of the total text was reproduced in Luke 4.

The Early Church

In the Apostolic Constitutions, the service of worship is ordered as follows:

> "Let the reader stand upon some high place; let him read the books of Moses, of Joshua the son of Nun, of the Judges, and of the Kings and of the Chronicles, and those written after the return from Captivity; and besides these, the books of Job and of Solomon and of the sixteen Prophets. When there have been two lessons read, let some other person sing the hymns of David, and let the people join at the conclusions of the verses. Afterwards let our Acts be read, and the Epistles of Paul our fellow-worker which he sent to the Churches under the guidance of the Holy Spirit; and afterwards let a deacon or a presbyter read the Gospels."[18]

In A.D. 140, Justin Martyr wrote the well-known account of the Sunday worship at Rome in his *First Apology* to the Emperor, Antoninus Pius. Justin describes the Sunday service as normally celebrated:

> On the day called the Feast of the Sun, all who live in towns or in the country assemble in one place, and the memoirs of the Apostles or the writings of the Prophets are read *as time permits*. Then, when the reader has ended, the President instructs and encourages the people to practise the truths contained in the Scripture

---

[18] Apostolic Constitutions II. 57, *Ante-Nicene Library*, xvii, p. 84.

lections [Emphasis added].[19]

The memoirs of the Apostles (surely meaning the Gospels and Epistles) and the writings of the Prophets were read for how long? For as long as time permits. But how long is "long"? And how much time does time permit? In Old Testament times, "long" meant that *an abundance of Scripture was read*, and time was simply the time necessary to read it.

"We assemble" says Tertullian, in his account of the practice of the Church in the second century, "to read our sacred writings....With their sacred words we nourish our faith, we animate our hope, we make our confidence more steadfast; and no less by the inculcation of God's precepts we confirm good habits."[20]

When one consults contemporary books on the subject of worship for the purpose of studying the element of Scripture reading, one will observe that usually there is only passing commentary regarding this topic, amounting to little more than a page or two. Even more striking is the fact that few have commented on what quantity of reading is appropriate for the worship service. Now, it may be that the necessity of the readings is automatically assumed, although that seems unlikely since the abuse of Scripture reading in worship is nothing to wink at. It is puzzling, nonetheless, that there appears to be such little argument in the vast majority of these theological books for the public

---

[19] William D. Maxwell, *An Outline of Christian Worship -- Its Development and Forms* (London, Oxford University Press, 1960), p. 12.

[20] Apol. 39, *Ante-Nicene Library*, vol. xi, p. 118.

reading of the Word of God.[21]

This is not a subject about which the christian ought to remain ignorant, for it is at the heart of his worship of Almighty God. When the congregation is uninformed about the significance of the Word, it will soon become apathetic, and the presence of God's Word will begin to wane. This darkness is becoming as evident today as it was in ages past. While a lectionary[22] was used in the Roman Catholic Church during the Middle Ages, the readings were in Latin, a language uncommon to most of the people in the pews. The people were fed "snippets" of Scripture; the Gospel and Epistle selections were often short, and did not encompass the entire New Testament. Old Testament passages were scarce. Not until the time of the Reformers was there an awakening that delivered the people out of spiritual bondage and neglect, and set their feet back upon the path of the enlightening truths of Scripture.

---

[21] A notable exception to this general trend is Louis DeBoer's chapter, "The Reading of the Scriptures," in *Worship in the Presence of God: A collection of essays on the nature, elements, and historic views and practice of worship* (Frank J. Smith and David C. Lachman, eds., Greenville, Greenville Presbyterian Theological Seminary Press, 1992), pp. 137-156.

[22] A. C. A. Hall, *The Use of Holy Scripture in the Public Worship of the Church* (London, Longmans, Green and Co., 1903). On p. 47, referring to Freeman's *Principles of Divine Service*, vol. ii, p. 415, he says, 'From the time of Pope Damasus (A.D. 400) the ecclesiastical writers first begin to refer to fixed lections from Holy Scripture.' Hall continues, "The *Comes* or lectionary was a well-known directory at the end of the fifth century, arranged either by St. Jerome (to whom it is commonly ascribed) or by some person of authority living in or near Rome about the same time."

REFORMED TRADITION

The Reformers of the 16th and 17th centuries reinstituted the Biblical practice of the reading of an abundance of Scripture in the worship service. When we take a look back in time, it is not difficult to see just how far many modern Reformed churches have deviated from Reformed practice regarding the reading of God's Word in public worship. In his *Works* (1523), Martin Luther describes the rites and ceremonies of the Wittenberg church. The Word of God was a treasure of God's grace for the persecuted in Luther's day. In a chapter entitled, "Formula of Mass and Communion for the Church at Wittenberg", Luther writes, "For by the mercy of God there is antidote aplenty among us through *the abundance of the Word of God*..." [Emphasis added]. In another chapter entitled "Concerning the Ordering of Divine Worship in the Congregation," Luther conveys his beliefs as to the manner of liturgical Scripture readings from the Old Testament, explaining what he means by an "abundance":

> ...this Lesson should be taken from the Old Testament in this fashion: One of the books should be selected and a chapter or two, or half a chapter, should be read until all of it has been used. After that another book should be selected, and so on, until the entire Bible has been

read through...[23]

The same men who wrote the *Westminster Confession and Catechisms* at the same time wrote a document entitled *The Directory for the Publick Worship of God; agreed upon by the Assembly of Divines at Westminster, with the assistance of Commissioners From The Church of Scotland*. This document sets forth the Traditional Reformed view of the reading of Scripture in the worship service in a section entitled, "Of Publick Reading of the Holy Scriptures":

> ...it is convenient, that ordinarily one chapter of each Testament be read at every meeting; and sometimes more, where the chapters be short, or the coherence of matter requireth it. It is requisite that all the canonical books be read over in order, that the people may be better acquainted with the whole body of the scriptures; and ordinarily, where the reading in either Testament endeth on one Lord's day, it is to begin the next. We commend also the more frequent reading of such scriptures as he that readeth shall think best for edification of his hearers, as the book of Psalms, and such like.[24]

In the 17th century, a combined effort was made by Puritans and Anglican Bishops to reform the liturgy of the Anglican church. Initial efforts were not successful due to certain Puritan exceptions to the lack of Biblical phraseology in the Anglican *Book*

---

[23]Martin Luther, *Works of Martin Luther*, Volume VI (Grand Rapids, Baker Book House, 1982), p. 61.

[24]Westminster Assembly (Glasgow, Free Presbyterian Publications, 1966), pp. 375-376. While there is no Scriptural proof for this precise amount or form, it does reflect the settled conviction of the Westminster divines as to what was appropriate.

of Common Prayer. However, in what has come to be known as *The Savoy Liturgy*, originally submitted as *The Reformation of the Liturgy* (1661), we find Richard Baxter's final expression of a more sure correspondence between worship and the Word of God. Hence the following concerning the use of Scripture in the worship of God:

> Then may be said the 95th, or the 100th Psalm; or the 84th. And next the Psalms in order for the day: and next shall be read a chapter of the Old Testament, such as the Minister findeth most seasonable... After which may be sung a Psalm, or the Te Deum said: then shall be read a chapter of the New Testament...[25]

Seventy-five years earlier the English Puritans had recognized the importance of the public reading of the Holy Scriptures, as well as the need at that time to establish a defined liturgical use of God's Word. In *The Middleburg Liturgy* (1586) written for use in Reformed churches, we find the following introduction:

> Upon the days appointed for the preaching of the Word, when a convenient number of the Congregation are come together, that they may make fruit of their presence, till the Assembly be full, one appointed by the Eldership, shall read some Chapters of the Canonical books of Scripture, singing Psalms between at his discretion: and follow, that so from time to time the holy Scriptures may be read throughout.[26]

During the exile in the Netherlands in the last decade of the 16th century, the worship of the left-

---

[25] Bard Thompson, Ed., *Liturgies of the Western Church* (New York, World Publishing Co., 1974, New American Library), p. 322.

[26] *Ibid*, pp. 391-392.

wing Puritans (also known as the Semi-Separatists) did not differ greatly from the usual Puritan order of service. A pastor of the church of Amsterdam who catalogued the order of worship recorded the following as "Item Number Two": "The Scriptures are read, two or three chapters, as time serves, with a brief explanation of their meaning."[27]

Because the Reformation restored the Bible to the people by translation into their native languages, the reading of the Scriptures took an honored place in the churches of Holland. The Synod of Wesel (1568)[28] ordained the following:

> ...that one or other elder or deacon, or someone else out of the congregation appointed thereto, should first read to the people one or two chapters for the congregation and furthermore that psalms be sung as is customary.[29]

---

[27] Horton Davies, *The Worship of the English Puritans* (Westminster, Dacre Press, 1948), p. 248. The author here refers to *John Robinson's Works*, Ed. Ashton, iii 485: The Catalogue of the Order of Service by Clyfton, the colleague of Johnson in the Pastorship of the Church at Amsterdam.

[28] An explanation of what is probably a more technically accurate title, and the reasons why, are found in the introduction to a Dutch work by P. Biesterveld and Dr. H.H. Kuyper (Professors at the Free University of Amsterdam), *KERKELIJK HANDBOEKJE bevattende de Bepalingen der Nederlandsche Synoden en andere stukken van beteekenis voor de Regeering der Kerken* (Kampen...J.H. Bos, 1905), translated into English in 1982 by Richard R. De Ridder as *ECCLESIASTICAL MANUAL including the decisions of the Netherlands Synods and other significant matters relating to the Government of the Churches*, p. 13.

[29] J. J. Van Oosterzee, *Practical Theology: A Manual for Theological Students*, "A Dutch Work Translated and Adapted to the Use of English Readers" translated by Maurice J. Evans (New York, Charles Scribner's Sons, 1878). It should be noted that Van Oosterzee sees this pronouncement to be in the course of the regular worship service. In his book he continues to explain this role, saying, "Very quickly, in country places at least, the task of prelector and precentor was

At the same time, however, this declaration reminded the appointed reader that he was to abstain from expounding on the Scriptures he read, "...in order not to put the sickle into another man's harvest, nor disturb the custom of the church by untimely explanations."[30]

It should be clear from these examples that the age in which we live consists of thousands upon thousands of unfortunate offspring of those who have committed the church to the wholesale destruction of the remembered past.

This is traditional Reformed worship: where the average amount of Scripture read in every worship service is two chapters. **This** is instituted Reformed worship: where, if the chapters are short, *more* than two chapters are read. **This** is historic Reformed worship: where all of the books of Scripture are read in order so that the congregation may become knowledgeable and familiar with all of the Scriptures. **This** is Reformed worship: where the cohesive parts of a liturgical order blend with, complement, but do not overshadow or detract from, one another. All of this implies the reading of an abundance of verses, and holds forth the importance of the distinct element of the reading of the Holy Scriptures in the worship of Almighty God.

---

entrusted to the schoolmaster, or one of his helpers" (p. 384).

[30]*Ibid*, p. 384.

SCRIPTURE READING AS AN ELEMENT OF WORSHIP TODAY

During the time of the Reformation, when God restored the preaching of the Word, the reading of the Scriptures and the preaching were often referred to simply as "the Word." Certainly the two are so closely related that they are mutually inclusive. The effectual hearing is brought about by the preaching, and the preaching is only faithful when supported and driven by the Scriptures. These days, however, it is not uncommon, even in churches which claim to be Reformed, to have as few as three or four verses of Scripture read in the worship service. Is it enough that three or four verses of Scripture are read? To most truly Reformed worshippers, this may seem a ridiculous question, the answer to which would be a resounding, "No!"

Nevertheless, there are some today who are of the opinion that the reading and preaching of the Word of God in public worship are not of primary importance. In his articles on the *Westminster Directory*, W. Robert Godfrey, Professor of Church History at Westminster Seminary in California, speaks of those having reservations about the public reading:

> How well do our churches measure up to this standard of the Directory? How much of the Bible is regularly read in our services? I suspect that very little of the Bible that is not directly related to the sermon is read in

most of our churches. Further I suspect that even the Scripture read before the sermon is getting shorter and shorter in many churches....Perhaps we think, "Must we listen to all those geneologies of people we have never heard of, all those laws that no longer apply, all those prophesies about nations long gone?" But we should ask ourselves, when we think that way, if we are really any different from liberals who remove from the Scripture passages that do not appeal to them."[31]

Jot by tittle, and tittle by jot, the Word of God is disappearing from the worship service. Why is this?

This sad situation is well described by Howard Hageman:

> But today we have a problem since the choice of Scripture is left entirely to the minister. This means that generally speaking the choice is determined by his homiletic intentions. In the old days, Scripture determined the sermon. We have nearly turned the thing around and let the sermon determine Scripture. But an even greater problem is posed by the fact that our system usually results in a distressingly small amount of the Bible's being read in the average congregation in any given year. Preaching often tends to cover a narrow range. Ministers often ride hobbies in their sermons. The result is obvious. And today when we have but one service a week in most places, and often but one lesson in that service, the situation is desperate, especially if we face the fact that such weekly exposure is the total acquaintance with Scripture that many of our people will have. As Reformed churchmen we must be aware of the dangers attendant upon any attempt to bind the Spirit of God. But at the same time, for a Church of the Word to have in its public worship but one selection of Scripture chosen arbitrarily from a small selection of the favorite books or even chapters of

---

[31] W. Robert Godfrey, from "Past Times - Reading Scripture," as it appeared in the *Outlook* (October 1991, Vol. 41, No. 9), p. 17.

one man is a situation which calls for correction. The use of the Bible in our liturgy must be more of a corporate matter than is the case at present.[32]

There are some modern worship services in which the integral element of Scripture reading is neglected, and as little as one verse is read! Such a practice is "justified" by the excuse that numerous verses are referenced, or even read, during the sermon. Now, we must ask a fair question: is this transfer a simple shuffling of incidentals for which we are granted liberty, or is it rather that essential elements of the worship of God are being stripped of their God-ordained importance, and their content and weight redefined by men? In his "Studies in the Shorter Catechism," Questions and Answers 51 and 52 on the Second Commandment, Gordon Reed, a Presbyterian minister, states:

> This commandment also requires that the Word be read and expounded. I was recently in a worship service in which a beautiful passage from God's Word was read. However, the sermon which followed had little if anything to do with that passage or any other passage from the Bible. On the other hand, I have attended worship services (yes, even Presbyterian worship services) in which **only one verse of Scripture was read in the entire service.** In both cases there was an absence of very necessary elements of worship [Emphasis added].[33]

---

[32]Howard G. Hageman, *Pulpit and Table: Some Chapters in the History of Worship in the Reformed Churches* (Richmond, John Knox Press, 1962), p. 123.

[33]Gordon Reed, from "Studies in the Shorter Catechism," as it appeared in the *Christian Observer* (April 6, 1990, Vol. 168, No. 14), p. 2.

In such cases where the sermon is pared down to make room for Scripture reading, the sermon itself, which is the teaching of God's people by the exposition of Holy Scripture — God's provision of food for His people's souls — is measurably reduced as well, thereby depriving God's people of the due instruction they need in order that they may be strengthened for the week ahead. The Scripture reading, on the other hand, is one of the essential parts for, by it, God Himself speaks to the congregation, and the congregation listens to His inspired and infallible Word without commentary! We are not to sacrifice one necessary element of the worship service to make more room for another. Such a practice can not be warranted or justified by the Scriptures, and it is not Reformed! Louis DeBoer's thoughts on the corporate reading of the Scriptures not only echo the sentiments of this study, but are worthy of quotation at length:

> The importance of reading the Scriptures cannot be overstressed. If one thinks that this is so obvious it need not be stated then one only has to study contemporary church practice to see the fallacy of that naive assumption...But as we have seen we are commanded to read the Word of God. If we crowd it out because we don't want to weary the people with a long service and the speaker doesn't want to surrender his time, then **we are dishonoring, displeasing, and disobeying God**. Reformed churches have a sound and Biblical tradition of giving adequate attention to the reading of the Word of God to the people. Most of them, if they dusted off their Directories for Worship, would discover that they are required to read a significant portion each service. Personally, I like to read two full chapters, one from each Testament, that go with the theme of the sermon. If the Word of God does not have an honored place in our services then we

are neither Biblical nor Reformed [Emphasis added].[34]

Why are three or four verses of Scripture now considered to be sufficient, when not long ago an entire chapter (and more) was read? Do solos, skits, slide presentations, liturgical dances and other extra-biblical substitutes convey the truths of God with as much fidelity and efficacy?[35] There seems to be a mindset surfacing in Reformed circles today which asks the questions, "Do we really need to read so much Scripture in the service when we have so many other means at our disposal to meet the needs of our people? After all, shouldn't we use other more effective means of *sharing Christ's love* in the worship service? Just how many verses *would* be enough, anyway? Do not these 'long' readings wear out the listener?" Again we quote from Godfrey:

> The readings must not be...so long as to wear out the listener. But how much wears out the listener? **Certainly not two chapters! If two chapters are wearying, then something is seriously wrong with the listener.** Listeners must not be lazy or let themselves slip into an "entertainment mode." They must work to listen attentively and eagerly to hear what God is saying to them [Emphasis added].[36]

---

[34]DeBoer, *op. cit.*, pp. 142-143.

[35]It is beyond the scope of this paper to address in depth the question as to whether or not such innovations have a place in the proper worship of God. Suffice it to say, they do not. God has given us no such commands in His Word, and with the absence of a positive Divine warrant, either expressed or implied, such novelties — as "creative" and "edifying" as they may appear to be — are strictly forbidden! See "The Regulative Principle Guides" earlier in this book (p. 11) for the basis of this.

[36]Godfrey, *op. cit.*, p. 17.

These questions may appear to be well-intended, but the Reformed believer must not be fooled by their innocent appearance. For underneath that sheepish appearance could be a wolf-like mindset which states: 1) God does not *really* work in people's hearts through the faithful reading and preaching of the Word, 2) worship should be celebrative, innovative and exciting, 3) the self-perceived "needs" of the people (however they are defined) can not be met by the mere reading and faithful preaching of the Word. We might not be surprised to hear these questions or statements from the members of a congregation, but we would probably be surprised to hear them from our church officers. Or *would* we be surprised? Like a frog lolling about a pot of cool water which ultimately boils to death because it is unaware that the water was ever so slowly being heated until it was too late to escape alive, perhaps these leaders have simply not perceived the gradual decline in the amount of Scripture read. Is it ignorance or willful intent? Either one has dreadful consequences.

Every element of an orderly worship service — the Scripture reading, the sermon, the prayer, the singing, and the sacraments — is a substantial and distinct part of the worship of God. Collectively, these elements constitute the whole of worship, but they are unique elements, and should be treated as such. They should be given no more, and no less, time or emphasis than is appropriate. Just what is "appropriate" is not to be conditioned or defined by the rash and changing whims of a Session or Consistory, a "Worship Committee," or the Pastoral staff. Practically speaking, we ought not to deviate from a suitable balance: a regard for the significance and rightful place of each integral part.

In Psalm 19:7-11, we find that the word of God is *"...perfect...sure...right...pure...clean...true and righteous altogether."* This Word is also spoken of as *"...the law...testimony...statutes...commandment... judgment."* Most importantly, God says of His Words that they are *"more to be desired...than gold, yea, than much fine gold..."* Do leaders in Reformed churches today desire the Word of God to this high degree, and yet remain satisfied with the reading of only three or four verses of Scripture in the worship service? Psalm 119:97 reads, *"O how love I thy law! it is my meditation all the day."* Do our church leaders love the Word of God to this extent, and yet remain content with the reading of three or four verses of Scripture in the worship service?

In Luke 24:27-32, we read of Jesus' encounter with two of His disciples on the Road to Emmaeus: *"And beginning at Moses and all the prophets, he expounded unto them in all the scriptures the things concerning himself... And they said one to another, Did not our heart burn within us, while he talked with us by the way, and while he opened to us the scriptures?"* How can our church leaders long for the hearing and faithful exposition of God's Word, and expect the hearts of their people to burn within them, when only three or four verses of Scripture are read in the worship service?

Psalm 78:4 says of the Scriptures, *"We will not hide them from their children..."* But for the sake of the children whose parents actually allow them to remain in the worship service: can our church leaders honestly claim that they are being faithful to such a standard, and that they are not neglecting these little ones, when only three or four verses of Scripture are read? Can they actually claim, as the Apostle Paul in II Timothy 3:15, that every child under their care and responsibility has *"known the holy scriptures, which are able to make thee wise unto salvation"*?

We are commanded of God to *"Search the scriptures..."* (John 5:39). God instructs us, *"Give ear, O my people, to my law: incline your ears to the words of my mouth"* (Psalm 78:1). He charges us, *"Study to shew thyself approved unto God, a workman that needeth not to be ashamed, rightly dividing the word of truth"* (II Tim. 2:15). Can our church leaders honestly say that they hunger and thirst for the Word of God, and have set their hearts upon such verses as these, when at the same time they remain content with the reading of three or four verses? (Needless to say, reading only three or four verses precludes the reading and hearing of the Law of God.) Can they claim to be a model of Mary in Luke 10:38-42, *"which sat at Jesus' feet, and heard his word,"* or are they more like her sister Martha, who was *"cumbered about much serving..."* and was *"careful and troubled about many things,"* but lacked in *"that good part that shall not be taken away"*? Do they not long for Jesus, the Word made flesh? Is there no heart of the Bereans in them, who *"...received the word with all readiness of mind, and searched the scriptures daily..."*?

WHY HAS THERE BEEN A DECLINE IN READING?

In the introduction to his book on public Scripture reading, Thomas E. McComiskey asserts his concern over the careless manner in which the reading is frequently performed. He explains:

> Perhaps one of the reasons for this is that public reading of Scripture is not emphasized in the practical theology departments of many of our major seminaries.[37]

In worship, some ministers show by their neglect of the Scripture reading that they think more highly of their own fallible interpretation of Scripture than of the hearing of God's Word itself. After all, they might reason, if the congregation views the minister's words as being no less important than those of the "human writers" of the Bible, "Why not place emphasis upon the living, rather than upon the dead, for is not a living dog better than a dead lion?" Again, we quote from DeBoer:

> Men, especially preachers, are often so infatuated with their own words that they give short shrift to the reading of the Word of God. It is typical in many churches for the minister to read a few, **a very few**, verses, his text, and then proceed right into the sermon.

---

[37]Thomas E. McComiskey, *Reading Scripture in Public* (Grand Rapids, Baker Book House), 1991, p. 9.

> If one is fortunate, he might actually stick to those few verses and give an exposition of them. All too often that is almost the last one hears of even those few verses....Christ himself taught in the Parable of the Sower that the word is the seed that bears fruit unto eternal life...It is a Scripture truth that if we sow sparingly we shall reap sparingly. If we would sow bountifully we ought to read the Scriptures in our services...It is not the eloquence of the preacher, it is not the appeal to fickle human emotions, it is not the logic of the sermon; but it is the Word of God itself that is the seed that bears fruit unto eternal life. If we really believe that, then we will never be sparing in the reading of generous portions of the word as we feed the flock of the Lord Jesus Christ when they assemble to hear it [Emphasis added].[38]

Unfortunately, it is through men such as these that God's people today have become ignorant of what the Bible and church history teach about Scripture reading. This is true of many other facets of worship as well. The Scripture reading may be seen as "just plain boring" in our day of "exciting" electronic media, and an unwelcome guest in a "church growth" entertainment model for worship. Other possible reasons for decline should be considered as well.

Modern Versions and Paraphrases

One has only to browse through a contemporary Christian bookstore to become aware of the proliferation of modern "translations" of the Bible. Most of these versions[39] have literally wrought

---

[38] DeBoer, *op. cit.*, pp. 142-143.

[39] **Perversions** is probably a more accurate term.

havoc in the Christian church today. Not only has the eloquence of the Authorized Version become unfamiliar to the contemporary reader and listener, but the feeble substitutes which in most cases rely upon inferior texts, and embrace higher criticism and dynamic equivalence, bring to the listener a paraphrased, impotent rendering which produces little heart-burning desire for God's Word (Lk. 24:32). There is little thrilling to the soul, and little longing for more. In the General Essays section of *The Literary Guide to the Bible* entitled, "English Translations of the Bible," Gerald Hammond concludes his analysis saying:

> At its best, which means often, the Authorized Version has the kind of transparency which makes it possible for the reader to see the original clearly. It lacks the narrow interpretative bias of modern versions, and is stronger for it...Through its transparency the reader of the Authorized Version not only sees the original but also learns how to read it. Patterns of repetition, the way one clause is linked to another, the effect of unexpected inversions of word order, the readiness of biblical writers to vary tone and register from the highly formal to the scatological, and the different kinds and uses of imagery are all, like so much else, open to any readers of the Renaissance versions, and best open to them in the Authorized Version.[40]

Red-letter editions of the Bible abound. As well-intended as the practice of emphasizing the words of Jesus may be, the result of this practice is that the rest of God's Word (also the Word of Jesus Christ) is de-emphasized, if not ignored. Some versions even colorfully highlight certain passages and

---

[40]Robert Alter, and Frank Kermode, Ed., *The Literary Guide to the Bible* (Cambridge, Harvard University Press, 1987), pp. 664-665.

phrases, thus accentuating the positive in order to eliminate the negative (e.g., Robert Schuller's *Positive Thinker's Bible*).

Also very common today on the pages of the Bible are man-inspired margin notes which can cause the uneducated Bible reader to question the reliability of the text, or even the legitimacy of entire sections of Scripture. Try to look up Mark 16:9-20 in the New American Standard (NASB) or the New International Version (NIV) for just one example of this. Then there are Bibles like the dispensationalist Scofield Bible which superimpose men's faulty interpretations and presuppositions onto the Scriptures with running commentaries on each page.

What does all of this have to do with the reduction in Scripture reading in the worship service? Directly, it has little to do with it, but indirectly it can cause a low and critical view of the Scriptures. But there *is* one significant factor which may be directly linked to this reduction: most modern versions contain *extra-biblical sub-headings within the text*, causing shorter, notated segments to advance to a greater position than the rest of the chapter, resulting in the reading and application of fewer verses. Such compartmentalizing of Scripture, which is very common in today's translations but foreign to the older versions, encourages the substitution of the shorter subtitled or emphasized text of the sermon for that of the main element of the Scripture reading. Hence the longer reading is thought to contain more "data" than the average listener can "process." It is therefore whittled down to size so that it might not "detract" from the message of the sermon.

In these and many other ways, modern Bible

publishers (some of whom are owned by secular corporations) and their "translator" henchmen have mutilated the two-edged sword so that it can serve as little more than a butter knife.

The Scourge of the Charismatic and Pentecostal Movements[41]

The Charismatic and Pentecostal movements must also be viewed as a contributors to the decline in the reading of the Word of God, for neither one is satisfied with the complete and all-sufficient revealed will of God (i.e., the Bible). Each one instead seeks to receive divine revelation (such as dreams, visions, tongues, messages from God, so-called "leadings of the Spirit," etc...) in addition to, and most often instead of and contrary to, the Bible alone and in its entirety. Hence, the Scriptures become less significant as compared to this "wallowing in the wind."

Such "wallowing in the wind," as prevalent as it is today, was seen in John Calvin's day as well. The following excerpts from Chapter IX of his *Institutes of the Christian Religion* testify to it:

> Furthermore, those who, having forsaken Scripture, imagine some way or other of reaching God, ought to be thought of as not so much gripped by error as carried away with frenzy. For of late, certain giddy men have arisen who, with great haughtiness exalting the teaching office of the Spirit, **despise all reading** and laugh at the simplicity of those who, as they express it, still follow the dead and killing letter.... What devilish madness is it to pretend that the use of Scripture, which leads the children of God even to the final goal, is

---

[41]Refer to fn #1.

fleeting or temporal? [Emphasis added][42]

> What say these fanatics, swollen with pride, who...carelessly [forsake and bid] farewell to God's Word, [and] no less confidently than boldly, seize upon whatever they may have conceived while snoring? Certainly a far different sobriety befits the children of God, who...are not unaware that the Word is the instrument by which the Lord dispenses the illumination of his Spirit to believers. For they know no other Spirit than him who dwelt and spoke in the apostles, and by whose oracles they are continually recalled to the hearing of the Word. [43]

The Acceptance of Unbelievers in the Churches

One more factor which may be responsible for the decline in Scripture reading in the worship of God, is the growing tendency for churches, through laxity or blatant error, to include in their membership and positions of leadership those who have no place, and those with whom the true child of God is to have no fellowship or communion. Thus, the unregenerate are appointed to teach in the church, lead programs in the church, and even *rule* as elders and deacons in the church. Yes, some of these "professionals" are in the pulpit as well! What can men such as these know of the things of God? How can they who are void of God's Spirit desire the milk and meat of the Word for themselves or their congregation, and respond positively to God's commands to obedience? For I Corinthians 2:14

---

[42]John Calvin, *Institutes of the Christian Religion*, Trans. Ford Lewis Battles, Ed. John T. McNeill (Philadelphia, The Westminster Press, 1960, Book I, Chapter IX, Section 1), p. 93.

[43]*Ibid*, Book I, Chapter IX, Section 3, p. 96.

says, "*The natural man receiveth not the things of the Spirit of God: for they are foolishness unto him: neither can he know them because they are spiritually discerned.*"

All of this corruption inevitably leads to a reduction in the corporate reading of — and belief in — God's Word. Where God's Word identifies sin, it will be denied and silenced. Where it proclaims God's wrath, it will be stifled. Where it sounds too negative, condemns with harsh clarity, divides families and friends, exhorts to holy and obedient living, or demands the crucifying of the flesh, it will be set aside and replaced with man-centered drivel nothing short of modern paganism. In the end, apostasy is assured, because the Truth has been set aside.

Such trends make the following Scriptures particularly applicable to today:

* Hosea 4:6: "*My people are destroyed for lack of knowledge: because thou hast rejected knowledge, I will also reject thee, that thou shalt be no priest to me: seeing thou hast forgotten the law of thy God, I will also forget thy children.*"

* Amos 8:11-12: "*Behold, the days come, saith the Lord GOD, that I will send a famine in the land, not a famine of bread, nor a thirst for water, but of hearing the words of the LORD: And they shall wander from sea to sea, and from the north even to the east, they shall run to and fro to seek the word of the LORD, and shall not find it.*"

Yet, the child of God may rest assured that all of these wicked attempts to limit and squelch the Scriptures — every denial, misuse and abuse of God's Word — will be remembered against those who have committed such crimes. The vanity of such efforts will be seen on the last day when this same Word will be held out as a testimony against them by the Living Word Himself, the Lord Jesus Christ.

Objections Considered
Pragmatism

A few objections might be offered at this point. First, it might be supposed that one factor determining the length of public reading at the time of the Reformation, and the generations immediately following it, is a pragmatic one: the lack of opportunity for people to read their own Bibles due to illiteracy and the relative unavailability of Biblical manuscripts, or the scarcity of printed Bibles.

But this supposition fails to take into account that while these unfortunate conditions may have existed at the time, nevertheless the people *did* have a grand opportunity for exposure to God's Word. We must remember that in those days, throughout the better part of Reformed Europe, there were up to three worship services on the Lord's Day, as well as services every day of the week! This certainly would have sufficed as provision enough for the people without causing the readings to be pragmatically extended as supposed.

Taking this one step further, it is easy to see how this supposed pragmatic argument may be arrived at. We live in a time when there is a high degree of literacy, and printed Bibles abound. Does this availability necessarily prove that God's people are reading all the more? Sadly, for many it is simply not the case. But even if it were, would these same people desire less reading of God's

Word in the worship service just because they had done a good amount of private reading during the week? On the contrary, one would think that they would desire the Lord's Word on the Lord's Day even more! Can one be thoroughly nourished by the meat and milk of the Word of God if only a snack is made available?

Adiaphora

Others might object that the length or amount of Scripture read is an **adiaphoron** – a thing indifferent, or neutral – and that the important thing is that a text, whether a lengthy narrative or a short phrase, be read and then carefully *explained* in its immediate context. It is said that in that way, God's Word will be central in our worship.

While the latter may be true, labeling the amount of Scripture read an **adiaphoron** is a bit simplistic. At the time of the Reformation, when the Scripture readings were long, there were great debates over certain religious practices (i.e. the wearing of vestments). These controversies over "adiaphora" dealt with whether or not those practices were things neither commanded nor forbidden by the Word of God, and if so, that they were matters that could be decided in the church by the mutual agreement of the ruling body. The strict Protestant view allowed only those things to be considered "indifferent" which did not impede the Gospel, but instead served the glory of God and the good of the church.[44]

---

[44]Richard A. Muller, *Dictionary of Latin and Theological Terms* (Grand Rapids, Baker Book House, 1986), p. 26.

Applying this strict definition to the matter of the amount of Scripture read in the corporate worship service, the establishment of longer readings in the days of the Reformation was a justifiable reaction to the practices at that time in the Roman Catholic church, with its shorter and language-barred (Latin) Scripture readings. Therefore, while these readings theoretically were **adiaphora**, to have continued in a practice that had an association with popery, their use would have become an obstacle to the promulgation of the Gospel, and hence would not have served the glory of God and the good of the church. This being a Puritan form of reasoning during that day, it is quite understandable that this concept was applied to arrive at the established directive for longer readings.

We are sure there are many in the Presbyterian Church in America (PCA) today who have great regard for the history of the Church, and who truly desire to be faithful in practice as well as in doctrine. We would call attention to the *Book of Church Order* (BCO) that governs the PCA. In the "Directory For the Worship of God" appears an accurate and wise summation of the truth. While this, of course, does not have the force of law in the PCA, and is not to be considered obligatory in all of its parts, it nevertheless states that it is an approved guide, and should be taken seriously as the mind of the Church agreeable to the Standards. In other words, the worship of a PCA church should have great regard for the reliability and trustworthiness of its own directions for worship. While only recommendations, they are highly Biblical. Before the leaders of a PCA church stray from this collection of wisdom of learned and faithful men, they had better be reasonably certain that their differing practices are justified.

Specifically, we find in BCO 50-4 that the direction given to the minister of God's Word is that the reading of Scripture should not be disproportionate to other elements of worship, nor *"rendered too short."*[45] Our desire is that many heed the warning against readings that are **too short**.

"Bibliolatry!" — The Bible An Idol?

There have been, however, isolated instances in Christendom when fear has risen against Scripture reading for its own sake, or the proclamation of God's Word by Scripture reading alone.[46] Today, arguments against the reading of an abundance of verses in the corporate worship of God arise from a lack of understanding, while others revolve around personal preferences, and the reasons given are often just plain sinful. There is, however, another objection that should be dealt with. It is not that this objection is in any way convincing or that it contains any great depth of thought. Moreover this objection is most likely to originate in neo-orthodox and liberal thinking rather than

---

[45]Presbyterian Church in America, *The Book of Church Order—The Directory for the Worship of God* (Atlanta, Committee for Christian Education and Publications, 1989), 50-4.

[46]On p. 131ff of his book entitled *Worship: Its Theology and Practice*, J.J. von Allmen says that "J.F. Ostervald in the eighteenth century strove hard to restore to the Reformed Church the proclamation of God's word by scriptural reading alone..." Also, on p. 56 of *Pulpit and Table*, Howard G. Hageman speaks of this same idea, namely that Scripture reading was used in a way that "it reflected the English Puritan horror of what was called 'dumb reading,' a dangerous relic of popery."

Reformed.[47] But it is considered here because it *is* an enemy to be dealt with, and the consequences of that system of thought can stand directly against the prominent place of *many verses* in the reading of God's Word. The accusation is brought that such a great preoccupation with *many verses* is idolatry, and that the Bible is made into an idol.

This argument supposes a violation of the First and Second Commandments:

> *And God spake all these words, saying, I am the LORD thy God, which have brought thee out of the land of Egypt, out of the house of bondage. Thou shalt have no other gods before me. Thou shalt not make unto thee any graven image, or any likeness of any thing that is in heaven above, or that is in the earth beneath, or that is in the water under the earth: Thou shalt not bow down thyself to them, nor serve them: for I the LORD thy God am a jealous God, visiting the iniquity of the fathers upon the children unto the third and fourth generation of them that hate me; And shewing mercy unto thousands of them that love me, and keep my commandments.*

One should be aware that because the practice of regular Scripture readings has been considered normative for the Christian church down through the ages, and Biblically supported as a practice of God's people in both the Old and New Testaments, the burden of proof for the above objection rests upon the accuser. He must demonstrate *from God's Word* that there has, in fact, been a violation. In order for the above argument to be justified, at least one of the following questions must be answered in the affirmative:

---

[47]The author, however, *has* on more than one occasion encountered and has been accused of this very thing by ruling elders of a Presbyterian church.

1) Is the reading of many verses serving other gods before the LORD God?
2) Is the Bible a graven image which man has made?
3) Is the Bible a likeness of anything in heaven, earth, or the water under the earth?
4) Does the reading of many verses cause us to bow ourselves down to the Bible and worship it?

All of these questions need further expansion, and become clearer when we understand what the Bible truly is. Regarding the first question, does the reading (or the Bible itself, for that matter) stand in distinct opposition to – or against – the LORD God, or is it instead intimately and uniquely associated with Him? Regarding the second question, is the Bible something made by man or made by God Himself? Regarding the third question, does the Bible resemble anything that God has *not* ordained to be made and used by man, or does it fall outside the scope of the prohibited likeness? And lastly, is the Bible bowed down to and served, or is it the God *of* the Bible which is being reverenced and worshipped?

To say that the Bible is the inspired and infallible Word of the Living God, which reveals His will for mankind, would probably be a sufficient answer as to the place it should have in the heart of God's people. But it is not only His will *for* us – it reveals the very persons of the Godhead *to* us.

John 1:1 says, *"In the beginning was the Word, and the Word was with God, and **the Word was God**."* This is not to say that, in some pantheistic fashion, God is a book, or He dwells in the Bible. He is the

Creator of all, He is the mighty God, Who is from everlasting to everlasting. But there is nonetheless a unique relationship between the written Word and the Incarnate Word, that in no way sets these two against each other. In true worship both are present. So we feel justified in saying that in this finite binding, the eternal God makes real to us by His Spirit an intimate association and communion through the hearing of infinite wisdom! This Word, then, is alive and powerful, and God speaks to His elect today just as directly as He did to generation after generation of His elect in times past — because it is the Living Word of the Living God. Therefore, we answer the first and fourth questions by saying that it is no other god but the LORD God we bow down to and serve when we show adoration for His Word, the Bible.

The second and third questions are answered quite easily from Scripture itself. We know that this Word *"...came not in old time by the will of man: but holy men of God spake as they were moved by the Holy Ghost."* And as to its being written and canonized to form the complete and all-sufficient Word: it was always God's intention to convey His Word in written form, and by His singular, providential care to preserve it down through the ages.

For we read of His instructions in Exodus 17:14: *"...Write this for a memorial **in a book**."* In Jeremiah 30:2 we read, *"Write thee all the words that I have spoken unto thee **in a book**."* And in Jeremiah 36:2: *"Take thee a **roll of a book**, and write therein all the words that I have spoken..."* In Isaiah 8:1: *"...Take thee a **great roll**, and write in it **with a man's pen**..."* And in Isaiah 30:8: *"...write it before them **in a table**, and note it **in a book**..."* In Habakkuk 2:2: *"Write the vision, and make it plain **upon tables**..."* And finally, in Revelation 1:11: *"What thou seest, **write in a book**, and send it unto the seven churches..."*

So, then, this argument against those who reverence the Bible and believe an abundance of Scripture should be read in the worship of God (i.e. that they violate the Second Commandment), is erroneous and without merit. It must be understood that having a great respect and even a great love for the Bible is really love of its Author. It is a love and adoration of God's revelation of Himself in the Scriptures. The very nature of the Bible and what is written therein testifies against such a rebellious claim. Rather, the First and Second Commandments are being transgressed by the very accusers themselves. It is *they* who have allowed something other than the Bible to take hold of their desires and respect. For, by raising their voices against an abundant exposure to God through the reading of His Word, they make themselves manifest before God as those who hate Him. Relinquishing the love of God's Word would surely cause this jealous God to visit *"the iniquity of the fathers upon the children unto the third and fourth generation."*

Indeed, it appears the Reformed Faith and short Scripture readings are strange and incompatible bedfellows! How many verses are enough? **MANY VERSES!** [48]

---

[48]The argument for "chapters" and "verses" has been primarily associated with declarations from the time of the Reformation. The history of chapter and verse division, particularly of the New Testament, is an interesting one. The purpose of the division was to facilitate reference. Chapter division is commonly attributed to Cardinal Hugo of Saint Cher (d. 1248), for use in his concordance to the Latin Vulgate. Others ascribe this to Stephen Langton, Archbishop of Canterbury (d. 1228) who made the division to facilitate citation. The present New Testament verses were introduced by Robertus Stephanus

AN EXHORTATION

It is hoped that this presentation of the Biblical and historical practice of reading the Scriptures in the public worship of God has educated those of us — both in the pulpit as well as the pew — as to its importance. While many ruling and teaching elders have not been *trained* to appreciate the importance of the public reading of God's Word, there are, unfortunately, a good number who disregard it, and lead their sheep astray through subtle means.

One significant indicator of a church's faithfulness is its practice of publicly reading the Holy Scriptures. In I Timothy 4:13, Paul charges the young minister to *"give attendance to reading..."* This exhortation may very well allude to public reading, as opposed to private reading, since in the same breath he enjoins Timothy to exhortation and teaching. In Colossians 4:16, speaking to the faithful brethren in Christ at Colosse, he says, *"And when this epistle is read among you, cause that it be read also in the church of the Laodiceans; and that ye likewise read the epistle from Laodicea."*

---

in his Greco-Latin Testament of 1551. The first English Bible printed with these chapters and verses was the *Geneva Bible* (1560). This explains why there are no Biblical accounts or early church directions as to how many chapters or verses of Scripture are to be read in the worship service. Certainly, an abundant reading of God's Word was desired in those times as well, but there was simply no means at their disposal to make explicit recommendation of the quantity of Scripture read.

A measurable and steady decline in the number of verses read may serve as a warning that a church is leaving its first love. Those of you who have perceived the subtle slithering of such a trend must not remain silent. It is your right to address your spiritual rulers. As you approach your session or consistory claiming to be suffering from a lack of heavenly food in God's house, the lack may be denied, and an attempt may be made to avoid the issue, and to portray your hungering as a spiritual deficiency, or an inability on your part to worship properly. They may question or impugn your motives, try to psychoanalyze your hearts, and labor to convince you with smiles and "loving" statements that you are wrong.

But you must be discerning, for Satan is the great deceiver, and many a tare "hath sprouted forth" not only in the pew, but in the pulpit as well. And these ordained vipers seek men of like nature to sit with them in the temple and stand in the Holy Place! You **must** openly resist this disease that has struck at the very heart of the church. You **must** fight valiantly for the Truth, for *"thy word is truth"*!

Let our cry be *semper reformanda!* Let us restore the disfigured and corrupted worship of today's churches to a form that bears the impress of Biblical principles and the Reformed Faith. Let us *"ask for the old paths."* Let God's people *"Seek ye out of the book of the LORD and read."* May the Word of God be faithfully preached, and may it always be abundantly read in the ears of the people.

> *"Blessed is he that readeth, and they that hear the words of this prophecy, and keep those things which are written therein: for the time is at hand."* (Revelation 1:3)

FINIS

APPENDIX

Historical Narrative And Debate At The Westminster Assembly Of Divines

Who should read the Scripture in the public worship of God, and should it be read with exposition? This is one of the many areas of debate that occupied the men of Westminster. Though not as extensive as other exchanges of the Assembly, it nevertheless was a subject about which men of faith did not find complete agreement.

The writings of the following three commissioners, present their best recollection and perception of the issue. In his *Letters and Journals* in the year 1643, Robert Baillie says the following:

> We had, as I wryte, obtained a Sub-committee of five to joyn with us for preparing to the great Committee some materialls for a Directorie. At our first meeting, for the first hour, we made prettie progress, to see what should be the work of ane ordinare Sabbath, separate from fasts, communions, baptismes, marriage. Here came the first question, about Readers: the Assemblie has past a vote before we came,

that it is part of the Pastor's office to read the Scriptures; what help he may have herein by these who are not pastors, it is not agitat. Alwayes these of best note about London are now in use, in the desk, to pray, and read in the Sunday morning four chapters, and expone some of the them, and cause sing two Psalms, and then goe to the pulpit to preach. We are not against the ministers reading and exponing when he does not preach; bot if all this work be laid on the minister before he preach, we fear it put preaching in a more narrow and discreditable roume than we would wish.[48]

In his *Journal of the Assembly of Divines* for Thursday, Nov. 2, 1643, John Lightfoot recorded the following:

The place in Ephes. iv. 11-13, cost some controverting upon Dr. *Temple's* doubt: but I proposing that the proposition which was intended to be laid in two parts, and the text supplied division to it, might be laid down jointly and in one piece; and accordingly it was suddenly done; and so we got out of a long debate, and came to the office of a pastor which was laid down thus:

The office of a pastor is, 1. Feeding; which is 1. Preaching, *i.e.* to teach. 1 Tim. iii. 3.

But before the entry upon this, Dr. *Gouge* tendered that there might be consideration had, whether the reading the Scripture be

---

[48]Robert Baillie, *The Letters and Journals of Robert Baillie, A.M.* (Edinburgh, Robert Ogle, 1841, Vol. 2), pp. 122-123.

not the pastor's office. And he proved it is from Numb. ix. Luke iv.

Mr. *Herle* backed the doctor's motion, and so did Dr. *Burgess*: and so we fell intentionally upon this point. Mr. *Seaman* conceived that this office did properly belong to the deacon.

Mr. *Wilkinson*, sen.: The Levites did read the Scriptures to assist Ezra; *ergo* he thought some young men fit for this purpose.

Mr. *Herrick*: A blind man may be a pastor; *ergo*, reading not necessarily the same office.

Mr. *Calamy* produced these places to prove there should be no reading without expounding: Eph. iv. God hath given gifts, *ergo*, we must use them; now reading requires no great gifts, 1 Pet. iv. 1.

Dr. *Temple*: Reading is preaching.

That by which faith may be begotten is preaching; but *ergo*, 1. Reading brings the glad tidings of salvation.

To this Mr. *Marshall* answered, That women and children may receive faith by reading; but they he hoped would not be called preachers.

Mr. *Bathurst*: Constantine Copronymus was converted by reading of Isa. xlvi.

Mr. *Herle*: Though reading may beget faith, yet is it not an ordinance, because not that promise upon it.

Mr. *Seaman*: The reading of the Word in reference to God is an act of worship; but in reference to the congregation, it is a means of edification; and in both these references the work belongeth to the pastor, but not necessarily to do it himself; yet not to any member of the congregation neither.

Dr. *Burgess*: 1. Public reading is an ordinance of God. Deut. xxxi. 11, Acts xv. 21, Ezra. 2. This public work ought to be by a public person only, and by one that hath commission from God to dispense this public administration. Deut. xxxi. 9,10, 1 Tim. iv. 13. 3. That whosoever performeth this, must be in commission to deliver the whole word by preaching as well as otherwise.

Mr. *Marshall*: The reading of the word in public is not an ecclesiastical office.

Mr. *Gibbon* proposed that the pastor and the reader might be two distinct offices.

Mr. *Palmer*: This office to be performed by none but by one deputed of God, Jer. xxxvi. Baruch.

Mr. *Calamy* out of Mr. *Hildersham*: The public reading is God's ordinance, and to be done by a public officer; and we may expect more a blessing upon it than upon the private reading.

Upon this subject we spent the whole day till two o'clock...And so we adjourned till morrow.

Continuing with Lightfoot's *Journal,* on Friday, Nov. 3, 1643:

Then fell we upon the work of the day, about the office of a pastor and...we fell upon that where we left yesterday, about public reading of the word. And this was agreed on on all hands: "That the public reading of the word is the ordinance of God." This then was inquired, "Whether a public minister is to do this, or any private one?" And here Dr. *Burgess* proved that Joshua's reading of the laws, Josh. viii.ult. was not by himself, but by his command; and for this he alleged Tostatus.

Dr. *Gouge* proposed that it might be ordered as a vote, that "reading of the Scriptures in public is the ordinance of God." Mr. *Nye* gainsaid the proposal, as not seasonable at this time.

Mr. *Wilson* interposed to have spoken to reading with or without exposition, which was awhile gainsaid; but at last being permitted, he said that:

1. There is no mention of reading without exposition, as Neh. viii. Luke iv. Deut. xxxiii. 10, Mal. ii. 7, Acts xiii. 15, xv. 21, 1 Thess. v. 27, Col. iv. 16, Heb. xiii. 22.

2. It belongeth not only to the pastor to read. When there was no singular call, there was some time a liberty to preach, much more to read.

1. Reading is not reckoned up as a ministerial gift.

2. It is no ministerial labour.

3. There is no reward promised for reading.

4. Reading is not a bare duty, but search the Scriptures.

5. There is no difficulty in this: and Paul saith Τίς ἱκανός.

I answered only the fourth of Luke, viz. That it is exceedingly mistaken: for that portion which was read by our Saviour, was not in any section in the prophets read through the year; *ergo*, that the lecture in the law and prophets was finished, and our Saviour chose this to preach upon.

Mr. *Gattaker* took at me; and I answered him at large.

And Dr. *Smith* took at him, and went about to prove that the reading of the Scriptures was not performed by the pastor, but by one ordained for the purpose; and this he proved out of Justin Martyr, who sets down these three distinct offices in the church, viz. and so likewise out of Austin, Cyprian, lib. ii. ep. 3. Canones Apostolorum.

Mr. *Nye*: The reading of the Scriptures is a distinct ordinance from preaching or interpreting them: but he also added, that in reading the Scriptures the reader, if he see just cause, may alter the English, if he be versed in the tongues.

Mr. *Bridges*: There is a standing ordinance: and occasional reading without exposition, or ability to expound: and he gave his sense, that reading with ability and liberty to expound is the standing ordinance, but not always actual exposition.

Mr. *Bathurst*: Deut. xxxi. 10. It was impossible the whole law should be expounded in so short a time. In Neh. viii. the exposition was out of Hebrew, which they had lost, into the Chaldee, which they understood.

Mr. *Goodwin*, out of Acts xiii. 15, proved reading without expounding; for there was first reading, then exhortation; and the sermon made there by Paul was not an exposition upon the law and prophets read, but a general treaty upon the whole story.

Mr. *De la March* held the reading of the word publicly to be a singular office; and for this he produced the use of some reformed churches.

Mr. *Wilson* did a little vindicate himself; after which was this vote:—

"The public reading of the word of God in the public congregation is a holy ordinance of God."

Then we had some large debate how to put our next question, "Whether this public reading be the pastor's office?" Mr. *Seaman* proposed it should go thus—"The pastor is to take care for the public reading of Scripture;" but it was utterly disliked.

Here Mr. *Reynor* desired a proof of this position, that this is the pastor's office; to this I answered, The epistles sent to the seven churches are directed to the angels to publish them.

When the thing was coming to the very question, it was much desired to delay the vote for fear of some inconvenience that might follow. And hereupon it was put to the question, whether this should be put to the question; and it was voted negatively; and so we laid it by for the present, and adjourned till Monday.

But before we had adjourned, Mr. *Palmer* moved, that to our former vote might be added this—"That public reading, &c. is a holy ordinance, though there be no immediate exposition of it:" but Mr. *Seaman* instanced that it might be disgraceful to us by misinterpretation. And this business cost us some debate, but at last coming to the question, it was voted affirmatively.

Continuing with Lightfoot's *Journal*, on Monday, Nov. 6, 1643:

> This morning being the first Monday in the month, our rules were read over, according to an order made for that purpose...Then fell we upon the report of the committee, viz. upon 1 Tim. iii. 2, 2 Tim. iii. 16,17, Titus i. 9, to be produced to prove that "it belongeth to the pastor's office to feed the flock by preaching," &c; but before we entered upon this, there came in the mention about the question, whether "reading the Scripture without explication belong to the pastor's office," and it was very long before we could resolve upon what to fall; and at last it was resolved by vote that this latter question should be resumed.
>
> Mr. *Reynor* first began to plead against the public reading to be the pastor's office. He questioned, 1. Whether the Levites did read in the synagogues: 2. If they did, whether they were fit pattern for pastors in the New Testament.
>
> Dr. *Temple*: That which is a divine public ordinance, belongs to the pastor's office; but this is so, *ergo*.
>
> Mr. *Bathurst*: Luke iv. 16. Our Saviour did customarily stand up to read.
>
> Mr. *Gibson*: 2 Cor. v. 19. The word is committed to the pastor, *ergo*, to read it as well as preach.

Mr. *Chambers* moved, that it might be resolved in some such clear terms, as might not tie it to the pastor only. This the Assembly thought needless, because that they laid the question, not whether the public reading of the Scriptures be appropriate, but whether it belonged to the pastor's office; and so it came to the question, and was voted affirmatively.

Then fell we upon the places of Scripture produced, 1 Tim. ii. 3, 2 Tim. iii. 16,17, Tit. i. 9; and they were voted without any doubting.[49]

In his *Notes of Debates and Proceedings of the Assembly of Divines and Other Commissioners at Westminster* for May 22-23, 1644, George Gillespie recorded the following:

By appointment of the Assembly, the Committee met for the Directory, to ask account of those to whom the several pieces were committed.

Mr. Young gave in his paper concerning the reading of Scripture.

Mr. Young's paper was approved.

I desired that that part might be left out where the Minister is directed not to expound till he have done with reading.

Mr. Goodwin and Mr. Ney said, Reading nakedly, without exposition, is an ordinance

---

[49]John Lightfoot, *The Whole Works of the Rev. John Lightfoot, D.D., Vol. 13: Journal of the Assembly of Divines*, Ed. Rev. John Rogers Pitman, A. M. (London, J. F. Dove, 1882), pp. 36-41.

of God, and that exposition should follow.[50]

Returning to Lightfoot's *Journal*, on Tuesday, June 11, 1644, we read the following:

> This morning Mr. *Marshall* reported the Directory for prayer and reading, being now drawn up and perfected, by the committee to which it was referred. I was not at the report, for I was waiting upon the House of Lords praying with them: when I came into the Assembly, I found them in debating of this point,—"Whether any may read the Scripture, in public, but only the pastor and teacher." Mr. *Palmer* was very urgent, that none might read but they. Mr. *Herle* backed him: but many spake against them. And this debate held us all the morning; and when we had all done, we laid it by till tomorrow.

Continuing with Lightfoot's *Journal*, on Wednesday, June 12, 1644:

> Our work to-day was where we left off yesterday; viz. upon this debate,—"Whether any one may read the Scriptures publicly, besides the minister:" this was canvassed 'pro et contra' exceedingly.
> Mr. *Palmer* stood exceedingly upon it, that none but ministers should: his main reason was this, Because the word read is

---

[50]George Gillespie, *Works: Vol. 2 - Notes of Debates and Proceedings of The Assembly of Divines and Other Commissioners At Westminster* (Edmonton, Still Waters Revival Books, 1991), p. 101.

the mouth of God to the people, and who is to be so but the minister? and where do we find any pattern in Scripture to the contrary?

The main arguments to the contrary were, that the burden would prove too heavy to the minister, if he must read all; and that probationers,—or, as they are called in the reformed churches, expectants,—that intend for the ministry, may supply this work for their initiation.—To this I assented, and shewed, that, in the New Testament, we find the preachers to be differing from the readers, as Luke iv. the Law was read before Christ preached on it. So Acts xiii.: and so Karraim among the Jews seemed to be the readers of the law, and the Pharisees, the expositors. This business held us all the morning, and when we had all done, it was referred again to the composure of the committee: and so we adjourned.

Continuing with Lightfoot's *Journal*, on Thursday, June 13, 1644:

>...Then fell upon the work of the day; viz. upon the business we had in hand yesterday. And first Mr. *Rutherford* produced 2 Kings ix. the example of a son of the prophets, or an expectant, that anointed Jehu: and by analogy, would conclude, that those that are among us, may read the Scripture.—This argument cost some debate: and so we fell upon the whole business in hand, and much 'pro et contra' was upon it: and, among other passages, Mr. *Gillespie* took up my argument, that I had yesterday,

about the Jews' having a reader of the law, and confirmed it out of Mr. Broughton: and he showed how he should cross reformed churches, if we would not admit of candidation. This debate held us all the day, with much agitation: at last it was put to the question in these words,—"It belongs to the pastor's and teacher's office publicly to read the word; yet such as intend the ministry, may occasionally both read the Scripture, and exercise their gifts in preaching in the congregation.—if allowed thereunto by the presbytery:" and it was voted to pass.

Continuing with Lightfoot's *Journal,* on Friday, June 14, 1644:

> This morning I was long attending on the Lords' House,—viz. till past eleven o'clock; but the work of the Assembly was the debating the Directory forward, about reading:—"How great a portion of the Scripture is to be read at every meeting, may be determined by the discretion of the minister; but we judge it convenient, that ordinarily one chapter of either Testament be read at such meeting, and sometimes more than one, when the shortness of the chapter, or order of the matter, requireth it:"—this was at last passed.
> Then also was debated, and voted, "We also commend the more frequent reading of such Scripture, as he shall, in his discretion, find best for the edification of his people,—as, the book of the Psalms, and such-like." Here I was absent, else I should

have excepted against the phrase of 'such-like.'[51]

The individuals presented above offer many ideas and refer to various passages of Scripture in defense of their positions. The reader is encouraged to search out these matters and study those passages for themselves.

---

[51]Lightfoot, *op. cit.*, pp. 282-284.

OLD PATHS PUBLICATIONS
Ernie Springer
223 Princeton Road.
Audubon, NJ 08106
609-546-4802

...ask for the old paths... Jer. 6:16

Old Paths Publications was established as a ministry for the cause of Christ and His Church. We seek to offer timely titles for the purpose of edification and instruction.

In our day, where true Christianity is increasingly under attack, *Old Paths Publications* will endeavor to bring together a united and confessional Reformed and Presbyterian thought, through the publishing of gospel truths given to us by the Spirit of God through His faithful elect, as they saw the fast approaching storm.

It is our hope and prayer that we may be of service to you, that our books might ring true to the Word of God, and that the Lord Jesus Christ might be exalted by all for His own glory.

THE FOLLOWING CLASSIC WORKS
ARE ALSO AVAILABLE FROM
OLD PATHS PUBLICATIONS

PASTORAL THEOLOGY
by Patrick Fairbairn

Rev. Fairbairn, a popular Scottish Presbyterian from the 19th century, had a sincere concern for the doctrine of the church and the relationship of its members. This classic work begins with his introductory remarks, a mere 38 pages, explaining <u>The Relation of the Pastoral Office to the Church, and the Connection Between Right Views of the One and a Proper Estimate of the Other</u>. *Rev. Fairbairn, author also of the popular book Typology, was a humble man who left instructions that no extended memoir of him should be published by any of his friends. A brief and succinct Biographical Sketch was, however, produced and is found at the beginning of* **PASTORAL THEOLOGY**. *This brief record of the life of one with high merits as an author, and noble Christian character, is well worth the reading.* **380 PAGES AND HARDBOUND WITH A DUSTJACKET WITH RARE PICTURE OF AUTHOR, AND SHRINKWRAPPED.**

Retail Price: $ 19.95 (Postpaid)

ORDER FROM

OLD PATHS PUBLICATIONS

A TREATISE ON SANCTIFICATION
by James Fraser

Rev. Fraser (of Alness) was a Scottish Presbyterian from the 18th century. From the very outset of his ministry he established a high reputation as a preacher, and was soon recognized as one of the most impressive and instructive preachers in a district where men of great and distinguished pulpit gifts were remarkably numerous. This 1897 edition of **A TREATISE ON SANCTIFICATION** *(originally The Scripture Doctrine of Sanctification) was the result of the careful collation by Rev. John Macpherson of previous printed editions with the original manuscript. A <u>foreword by Dr. Sinclair B. Ferguson of Westminster Theological Seminary</u> and an interesting 20 page Biographical Sketch precedes what is avowedly a doctrinal commentary on Romans 6, 7 and 8:1-4. These chapters are themselves doctrinal, expressly devoted to the exposition of the Scripture Doctrine of Sanctification. The commentary deals with each chapter giving a careful introduction to each, treating of the general scope and contents of the chapter, and especially combating defective or erroneous views of the standpoint and intention of the apostle. Each verse is commented on separately, and the results of this exegetical study are then given in a paraphrase. This doctrine of sanctification is a subject critical to the Christian's understanding in every age, especially in our twentieth century where carnality has run rampant.* ***A MUST purchase*** *for those striving for sanctified living.* **525 PAGES AND HARDBOUND WITH A DUSTJACKET WITH RARE PICTURE OF AUTHOR.**

Retail Price: $ 29.95 (Postpaid)

ORDER FROM

OLD PATHS PUBLICATIONS

REVEALED TO BABES: CHILDREN IN THE WORSHIP OF GOD
by Richard Bacon

Christians must follow the teachings of Christ and the Scriptures. This seems plain in and of itself. But do we truly apply this principle of the Christian life to our worship when it concerns the place of our covenant children? Does the Bible tell us who our covenant children are and does it give us commands as to their need for worship? What did Jesus have to say about the presence of covenant children in worship? Man's chief end is to glorify God and enjoy Him forever. We do this especially in the public worship where God's covenant people assemble to hear His Word. The children of the church are not excluded from that chief end. Richard Bacon deals with these questions and more. He is thorough, and conclusive in his approach to this subject, and clearly demonstrates from the Scriptures that children do belong in the public assembly of God, that they have certain rights as well as certain duties before the Lord that must be maintained. While the commands of Scripture require obedience from all who sincerely take the name of Jesus upon their lips, Presbyterian and Reformed Christians, by reason of their Confession, Church Order, and Reformation heritage, have an even greater responsibility to stand behind their profession. As Rev. Bacon states, "It is time for Presbyterians to become consistent with the theology of the Bible and to put into practice the theology that they claim to believe." **75 PAGES.**

Retail Price: $ 7.95 (Postpaid)

ORDER FROM

OLD PATHS PUBLICATIONS

THE REVIVAL OF THE ECCLESIASTICAL TEXT AND THE CLAIMS OF THE ANABAPTISTS
by Theodore P. Letis

During the Sixteenth century religious renewal movement which began in Germany and spread in time throughout all of western Europe, an extreme element took Martin Luther's teaching to abusive lengths. In so doing, these radicals nearly jeopardized what today we know as the great Protestant Reformation. Thinking Luther, Calvin and Cranmer had not gone far enough, many of these Anabaptists advocated political revolution as the means for bringing in what they perceived to be a restorationist Christianity. Today, this same radical spirit lives among many groups in North America who hold extreme views regarding the Authorized Version of Scripture. This essay puts this present controversy in its historic context. 54 PAGES AND 13 WOODCUTS.

Retail Price: $ 7.95 (Postpaid)

ORDER FROM

OLD PATHS PUBLICATIONS
Exclusive North American Distributor
for the
Institute for Reformation Biblical Studies